FLYING IN A HOT AIR BALLOON

FLYING IN A
HOT AIR
BALLOON

by Cheryl Walsh Bellville

 Carolrhoda Books, Inc./Minneapolis

Carolrhoda Books, Inc.
A division of Lerner Publishing Group
241 First Avenue North, Minneapolis, MN 55401 U.S.A.

Website address: www.lernerbooks.com

LIBRARY OF CONGRESS CATALOGING-IN-PUBLICATION DATA

Bellville, Cheryl Walsh.
  Flying in a hot air balloon / by Cheryl Walsh Bellville.
    p. cm.
  Includes index.
  Summary: The author describes her experiences with hot air
ballooning as passenger and ground-crew member and depicts
the sport from flight preparation to dismantling.
    ISBN 0-87614-750-3 (lib. bdg.)
    1. Ballooning—Juvenile literature. [1. Hot air balloons.
2. Ballooning.] I. Title.
GV762.B45 1993
797.5'1—dc20   92-37390

Manufactured in the United States of America
3 4 5 6 7 8 – GPS – 05 04 03 02 01 00

The author wishes to thank Matt Wiederkehr, Mary
Aamodt, Don Piccard, and Jim Stegbauer for their help
with this book. Very special thanks to Patti Mogren and
Sue and Dave Johnson. This book wouldn't have happened
without you!

Additional photographs courtesy of: the Smithsonian
Institution, p. 15; Jim Stegbauer, pp. 28–29; Dave Johnson,
p. 30.

Metric Conversion Chart

When you know:	Multiply by:	to find:
pounds	.45	kilograms
feet	.3	meters
miles	1.60	kilometers
degrees Fahrenheit	.56 (after subtracting 32)	degrees Celsius

For Katey, Erin, Kimi, and Megan—
four adventurous girls

I've always loved flying. I've flown in huge planes and tiny planes, antique planes from World War I and very modern planes controlled by computers. Usually I'm a passenger on these flights, but sometimes I'm the pilot. Still, I'd never thought of flying in a hot air balloon until my friend Patti invited me to ride with her.

Patti has been a hot air balloon pilot for several years. Every summer she flies her balloon in many **rallies** and local festivals. The balloon rally she invited me to was part of a summer celebration called River Days, in Hastings, Minnesota.

The day of the rally, I rode with Patti and the four members of her **crew** to the balloon site. Our van pulled a small, flat trailer that held the balloon and the equipment for the flight. On the way to Hastings, Patti and the crew told me stories about other balloon rallies. Telling these old stories and talking about today's rally had the crew excited by the time we drove the van and trailer onto the grassy field where we would launch the balloon. I was excited too, even though I didn't know what to expect.

Our experienced ground crew knew its job and went right to work, while I walked around taking pictures. First, they took a large wicker basket called a **gondola** (GAHN-duh-lah) off the trailer and set it on its side on the ground. The gondola is the part of the balloon that the pilot and passengers ride in.

Next, the crew unloaded a large cloth bag that held the **envelope** of the balloon. The envelope is the part that holds the air. It looked pretty heavy. Patti told me it weighed about 170 pounds—which is about as heavy as an average man. The crew took the envelope out of its storage bag and carefully spread it out full-length on the grass. Then they attached the envelope to the gondola with cables.

A crew member prepares to connect the burner to the gondola (left). A small box inside the gondola (below) holds the flight instruments. The dial on the left is the variometer, the window in the center is the altimeter, and the dial on the right is the pyrometer.

Finally, the crew fastened a burner to the top of the gondola. This burner heats the air inside the envelope, and the heated air lifts the balloon off the ground.

Patti's flight instruments were already in the gondola. The **altimeter** (al-TIM-muh-ter) measures the distance between the balloon and the ground, the **pyrometer** (py-RAH-muh-ter) measures the temperature of the air inside the envelope, and the **variometer** (va-ree-AH-muh-ter) measures the speed at which the balloon moves up or down. All balloons are required to carry these three instruments. Patti also keeps her propane fuel tanks and a fire extinguisher on board.

As the crew worked, Patti carefully checked every step of the preflight preparations. When all the parts of the balloon were in place and everything was connected and secured, the crew began the next step: inflation.

Friends who had come to watch the rally joined us to help inflate, or fill up, the balloon. Two crew members held open the **mouth,** or opening, of the envelope while someone else set a fan alongside the gondola, where it could blow air into the envelope. The fourth person held a rope that was attached to the **crown,** or top, of the envelope. This rope is called the **crown line.** Holding the crown line keeps the balloon from rolling from side to side when it begins to fill with air. It also keeps the envelope in line with the gondola. If the balloon weren't held steady, the moving envelope could get in the way of the burner's flame, and the mouth of the envelope would be scorched. For the same reason, the burner always faces the same direction the wind is blowing during inflation.

One of the balloons taking part in this rally was a replica, or copy, of the very first balloon to carry people aloft. This balloon, the *Montgolfier*, was named after two brothers, Etienne and Joseph Montgolfier, who lived in France over two hundred years ago. They noticed that in their fireplace, smoke always rose upward from the fire. They wanted to know if smoke would make objects rise.

So they set up experiments in which they trapped smoke in small paper and cloth bags, and just as they expected, the bags floated upward. The Montgolfiers made these bags larger and larger, and soon they discovered that the more smoky air these bags, or balloons, held, the higher they rose. The Montgolfiers also discovered that these larger balloons could carry weight.

Eventually the Montgolfiers decided to try to carry passengers in one of their balloons. The first hot air balloon passengers were not people, they were animals: a duck, a rooster, and a lamb. When these passengers came back to earth unharmed, the Montgolfiers sent two men up, Pilatre de Rozier and the Marquis d'Arlandes. These two men were the first people to fly in an aircraft. Like other early balloonists, they had to carry straw and other materials on board to create the smoke needed to keep the balloons aloft. Since then, we've discovered that heat, not smoke, makes a balloon fly. When heated, air expands, or spreads out, so hot air is always lighter than the same amount of cool air.

In 1783, the Montgolfier *became the first balloon to carry people aloft.*

Soon after the Rozier-d'Arlandes flight, people began using a gas called hydrogen to fill balloons. In these gas balloons, pilots didn't have to carry extra fuel on board, because all the hydrogen needed for the flight was sealed inside the balloon before it lifted off. Hydrogen gas makes balloons rise because it's lighter than the air surrounding the balloon. And although people knew hydrogen balloons could catch fire from a single spark, they felt hydrogen was safer than the open fires in hot air balloons.

Later, helium gas was also used to fill gas balloons. Although helium is safer to use than hydrogen, it is very expensive. These days, a single helium flight costs about $2,000.

In the early 1950s, the United States Navy decided to find a cheaper way to fuel balloons. They turned back to hot air balloons for a solution. In 1953, over 150 years after the first hot air balloon flight, the United States Navy developed a heater, or burner, fueled with propane gas. The propane burner provided a safe way to heat the air inside the envelope. Most importantly, it saved money. These days, a hot air balloon flight fueled with propane costs only about $35.

Suddenly, a large number of people could afford to fly in hot air balloons. The invention of the propane burner is the most important reason for the current popularity of ballooning.

The thrill the Montgolfiers felt watching the first passenger balloon flight can't have been much different from what I was feeling that day in Hastings as I watched the hare balloon lift off and move away from the launch site. The other balloon crews hurried to get their balloons into the air. Blasts from burners roared around me as other balloons began to stand up. They looked enormous at such close range. Most of the balloons in the rally were sixty feet tall—about as tall as a five- or six-story building.

When our balloon was inflated to a rounded teardrop shape, Patti fired our burner too. As the air inside the envelope became warmer than the air outside, the envelope expanded and began to lift off the ground.

While our ground crew held on to the edge of the gondola, our big red balloon stood upright. Standing just below it, I tipped my head back as far as I could, to see the huge shape swaying slowly above us. The sight was so amazing, I almost forgot I was a passenger.

Suddenly I heard the crew yelling at me to hurry into the gondola. I climbed in as fast as I could, and Patti gave the "hands off" signal to the crew. They took their hands off the edge of the gondola, and I leaned down inside to change to another camera. Before I could look out over the edge again, I discovered that we had risen about three hundred feet into the air—without any feeling of motion! We had risen through the air like a bubble rising through water, and just as quietly.

The afternoon was hot and hazy. The warmer the temperature is outside the envelope, the warmer it must be inside, so Patti had to use the burner a lot in order to gain **altitude,** or height above the ground. The day we were flying, the temperature outside was 85° F. Inside the envelope, it was over 200° F.

An irrigation, or sprinkler, system created a pattern of circles in this field.

When we reached the altitude Patti wanted, she used the burner less often, and we leveled off. We flew past the river bridges and over the town to the farmlands beyond. No wind blew on my face, because we were moving along with the wind, not into it as you do in an airplane. There was nothing between us and the countryside below except the basket we stood in and the ropes and cables connecting us to the envelope above. The only sound we could hear was the blast of the burner.

Looking ahead, I saw that we would be passing over a herd of cattle. Patti gave the burner another good blast. She wanted to gain altitude so that the sight of the balloon and the sound of the burner wouldn't startle the cattle. A long way off, we could see two other balloons that seemed to hang in the sky.

Below us, the roads and farms made wonderful shapes and patterns. I could see members of our ground crew—now our chase crew—in the blue van, following our route. Chase crews always include at least two people. One person drives, and the other person watches the balloon and gives directions to the driver. Our chase crew had packed the fan into the van after we lifted off. Then they got into the van and followed our flight. Patti talked with them through a two-way radio. She told them where she saw roads they could take to stay on our flight path.

We'd lost sight of the hare balloon and decided not to continue looking for it. Instead, we started to look for a good place to land. I was enjoying the flight so much, I could have kept flying forever. I knew, however, that balloonists must land before it gets dark. After dark, power lines and other obstacles can make flying and landing a balloon dangerous.

There weren't any big landing spaces near us, so Patti decided to land in a small hay field she saw in the distance. It lay wedged closely between two cornfields, but she thought we could land there without difficulty. She radioed the chase crew and gave them directions to the field so they could ask permission for us to land there.

Patti pulled a cord to open the **maneuvering vent** on the side of the envelope. The vent allowed the heated air inside the envelope to escape, and slowly we began to lose altitude. I watched as the large rectangles of the fields became individual rows of corn. As we dropped lower, the rows became individual stalks of corn.

Patti guided the balloon toward the narrow hay field and told me to face the direction we were landing. She showed me how to hold on to the edge of the gondola and bend my knees to absorb any shock from the landing.

The edge of the gondola bumped lightly on the ground, and we were down. A balloon, unlike an airplane, has no wheels, so it can't use a runway to slow down when it lands. If there is much wind, a gust may catch the balloon and drag the gondola along the ground. That day the air was fairly still, and we set down gently and stayed put.

We'd landed deep in the fields of a farm near Hastings. Our crew had a hard time figuring out which farm owned the field we were in and how to get there from the road. We had already deflated the balloon and spread it out on the ground when they reached us. The crew packed the envelope into its bag while Patti disconnected the cables and burner from the gondola.

Finally, the envelope and the gondola were back on the trailer. The crew surrounded me, laughing, as Patti poured a glass of champagne on my head to mark my first balloon flight.

The tradition of champagne goes back to the very first balloon flights in France. Because a hot air balloon coming out of the sky was such an unusual sight in the 1700s, people in the French countryside thought the balloons were from outer space. So these early balloonists carried bottles of champagne with them to prove they were from earth.

As we celebrated, I looked up to see another reminder of the early days of ballooning, the *Montgolfier*, fly silently past. My first balloon flight was behind me, but I knew it would not be my last.

Obviously, many people have had the same reaction to ballooning that I did. Hot air ballooning is popular all over the world, and the number of people flying balloons grows every year. People sometimes fly their balloons alone. Sometimes they fly in organized rallies like the one I was in. These rallies may be small, with only a few balloons participating, or huge, like this one in Albuquerque, New Mexico (left). Albuquerque hosts the largest hot air balloon rally in the world. In 1992 over 650 balloons were entered.

A large balloon rally like the one in Albuquerque is a good place to see the wonderful variety of styles and colors of hot air balloons. Balloon owners design their own colors and patterns. Each balloon is one-of-a-kind and easily identified by other balloonists.

At a rally, the bright colors jump against the sky. Some balloons have fringes or flags flying from their envelopes. A few are decorated with **bunting,** fabric that is draped around the outside of the balloon. Others have advertisements on them. Some balloons are not even round, but are shaped like such things as a high-top tennis shoe or Donald Duck.

29

Balloon rallies can be international, national, regional, or local. They take place in every kind of landscape and during every season of the year. In the United States, one of the most popular places for ballooning is Alaska, a state with long, snowy winters and wild countryside. Any place will do, as long as it has the two requirements for a successful balloon flight: an open spot to land and a road to reach the landing site.

A frozen lake makes a good place for a balloon launch.

Organizations all over the world support the sport of hot air ballooning. Some are small local organizations and clubs, and others, such as the Balloon Federation of America (BFA), have thousands of members nationwide.

The BFA is associated with the Federal Aviation Administration (FAA). The FAA sets the rules for flying all kinds of aircraft in the U.S. and inspects all aircraft to make sure they are safe to fly. The FAA also has approved several schools for hot air ballooning. These schools prepare students for private and commercial pilot's licenses.

The BFA and other ballooning organizations publish newsletters that give balloonists safety tips and technical information about flying hot air balloons. The newsletters also tell about ballooning activities and print advertisements for people interested in buying or selling balloons and ballooning equipment.

Other ballooning organizations are more like social clubs. They organize rallies and other social events that bring balloonists together for fun and sometimes for competition.

Aaron, Katey, Dave, and Sue attach the burner to the gondola.

The next time I was invited to see a balloon flight was late in the summer. The *Montgolfier* replica was being piloted by Dave Johnson. Dave and his wife, Sue, had studied old books and drawings of the original *Montgolfier* and adapted the design in order to make a modern hot air balloon. Dave painted symbols of the zodiac, an ancient calendar, onto yellow fabric. Sue sewed this fabric to the blue nylon envelope.

Dave and the *Montgolfier* were taking off with three young passengers: his children, Aaron and Stephanie, and my daughter, Katey. The three children were not only passengers on the flight, they were also the ground crew. Aaron and Stephanie had flown with their parents many times before, but this was a new experience for Katey.

Earlier in the day, Dave called the weather service to see if the day would be good for a flight. The weather service said it would be mild and pleasant with very little wind. This was just the kind of day Dave had hoped for. But he checked with the weather service again just before leaving for the launch area to be sure that no storms were moving into the area and the wind speeds hadn't changed. If there had been winds over eight miles per hour either on the ground or at the altitude he planned to fly, or if any storms had been nearby, this flight would have been postponed until another day. Once he is aloft, Dave depends on his experience as a balloon pilot to notice changes in weather conditions.

Katey and Aaron hold open the mouth of the balloon while Stephanie aims the fan at the opening.

As we were inflating the balloon, a car drove up. It was Dave's brother Loren and his children, Spencer and Natalie. Loren said he would help too, so I was free to be an observer again.

I walked around the balloon, taking pictures and watching it change size and shape as it filled with air. When I looked into the mouth of the partially filled balloon, I was surprised at how beautiful it was inside. The sunlight coming through the blue envelope gave me the feeling of being underwater. Loren and his children were dark shapes against the fabric of the balloon as they stood outside, watching it grow larger.

The view into the envelope from the crown (top) and the mouth (bottom)

When the envelope was about three-fourths full, Dave fired the burner and began heating the air inside. Natalie wanted to ride in the balloon, but Dave thought she was too small. No one wanted to disappoint her, so she was given a special ride called a **tethered flight.** This means that the balloon is tied to the ground by ropes so it will not fly away.

After Natalie's tethered flight, her father lifted her from the gondola. Then the lines that held the *Montgolfier* to the ground were unhooked, and the beautiful blue balloon floated upward.

Spencer and Natalie waved to Dave and the older children. Dave waved back and shouted good-bye, but the children didn't see us. They were busy watching shrinking buildings and roads below them as they drifted toward the countryside. I remembered how wonderful it was to see out around me from so high above the ground, and I wished I could be in the balloon with them.

Once the balloon was up, Sue, Loren, Spencer, Natalie, and I became the chase crew. We got into the pickup and car and followed the balloon. I rode in the pickup with Sue. My job was to watch the balloon and look for roads that would keep us near the balloon's path. I told Sue when I thought the balloon was changing direction or moving away. Loren and his children followed us.

A short distance down the road, Sue pulled over to talk to Dave on the two-way radio. Loren pulled over too, and Natalie and Spencer got out and waved at the balloon. This time, the children in the balloon saw us and waved back.

But we had a problem. The radio was not working. This happens sometimes, and Sue wasn't worried. She and Dave flew together many times before they began using radios to communicate with their chase crew. We would use the old way instead, and just keep watching and following.

After deciding what direction the balloon was drifting, we got back into our vehicles and continued to follow it. The balloon wasn't moving very much. Sue said that they were **becalmed,** which means that there is no wind to move the balloon. It was hanging motionless in the still air.

Dave gave the burner a blast to make the balloon rise. He was hoping to find an air current that would move the balloon sideways. There wasn't one, so he released some air from inside the balloon by opening the maneuvering vent. Maybe down lower they would find more air movement. He didn't find an air current there either, so they rose to their original altitude and waited. Soon we felt a breeze, and the *Montgolfier* began to move again.

The afternoon was lovely, but it was getting late. The balloon seemed to be sinking as I watched it from the moving pickup. Then I noticed that the bunting on the *Montgolfier* was beginning to billow up, a sure sign that the balloon was coming down.

Dave aimed for the center of a harvested cornfield. He wanted to land a good long distance from the road so that if a sudden wind came up, the balloon would not be blown into power lines.

As the balloon descended, I could see Stephanie and Katey leaning over the edge of the basket, watching the ground get closer.

We parked close to the field, and Loren and Sue ran to grab the balloon when it landed. As soon as it touched down, the three children scrambled out of the gondola to help. Dave stayed inside to keep the balloon inflated, while they carried the balloon back to the road. It was not heavy because the air inside the envelope was still much warmer than the outside air. Dave used the burner a couple of times as he was carried along, so that the balloon would stay upright.

When we reached a good place to deflate, he pulled the **rip cord,** and the huge balloon began to collapse. Dave and Sue laid the gondola on its side, and everyone ran to get out of the way of the falling balloon. The **rip panel** on the top of the envelope was completely open so that it would lose air quickly.

Katey and Stephanie hold the crown line as the balloon is deflated. This is not hard to do, because the balloon doesn't move much.

Katey and Stephanie had fun leaning back against the pull of the crown line. Their job was to keep the envelope stretched out in a straight line so it would be easier to pack.

The Johnsons' friend Mr. Christianson came by just in time to help Dave and Aaron squeeze the last of the air from the balloon. Starting at the crown, Stephanie, Katey, and Sue packed the envelope back into its bag, and another good day of ballooning ended.

Sue and Dave gave Katey a certificate to help her remember the day. It had this poem on it:

You ascended today in voyage,
detached from earth
yet in full harmony with it.
So enjoyable was this great experience
that the winds welcomed you with softness…
and the sun blessed you with warm hands.
You flew so high and so well
that God joined you in your laughter
and set you gently back again
into the loving arms of Mother Earth
(and your friends).

Back at the launch area, the Johnsons dropped off Katey and me at our car. We called out many thanks for such a wonderful day. The sun was setting as we drove home to bed and dreams of flying above the world in a hot air balloon.

Glossary

altimeter: an instrument for measuring the distance between an aircraft and the ground

altitude: the height at which an aircraft is flying

becalmed: motionless because of a lack of wind

bunting: fabric draped around the outside of the envelope for decoration

crew: the group of people responsible for helping set up and take apart a balloon

crown: the topmost part of the envelope

crown line: the rope attached to the top of the balloon, used to keep the envelope aligned with the gondola during inflation and deflation

envelope: the part of the balloon that holds the hot air, usually made of nylon fabric

gondola: the part of the balloon in which passengers stand, usually made of wicker

maneuvering vent: a flap on the side of the envelope that can be opened to release hot air a little at a time

mouth: the round opening at the bottom of the envelope

pyrometer: an instrument for measuring the temperature at the crown of the balloon

rally: a gathering of balloonists for fun or competition

rip cord: a rope, attached to the rip panel, that the pilot pulls to let all the air out of the balloon

rip panel: a large flap located at the crown that, when opened, rapidly releases the air from the envelope

tethered flight: the act of standing in the gondola of an inflated balloon while the balloon is securely tied down. The balloon floats as much as 100 feet above the ground and sways slightly with the wind, giving the feeling of flying.

variometer: an instrument for measuring (in feet per minute) how quickly an aircraft is rising or falling

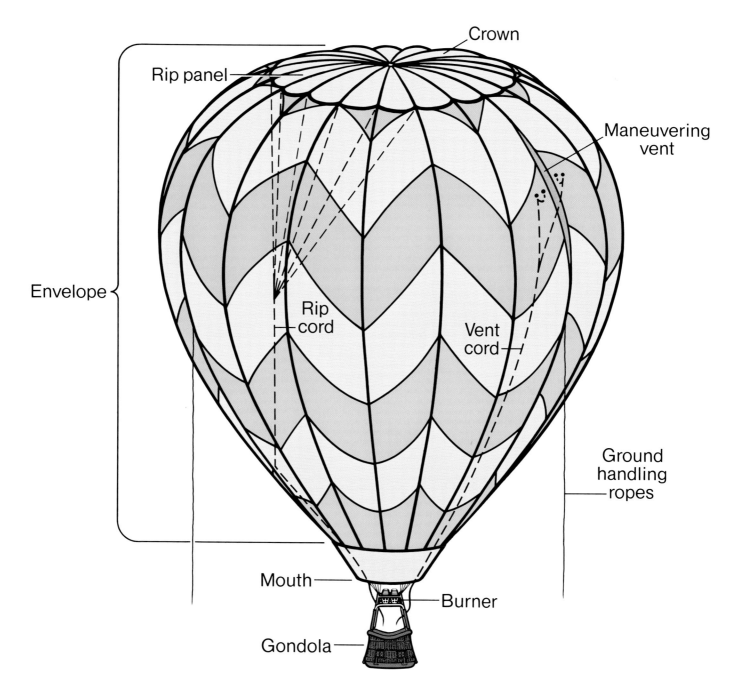

Crown

Rip panel

Maneuvering vent

Envelope

Rip cord

Vent cord

Ground handling ropes

Mouth

Burner

Gondola

47

Index